Is this
a joke?

No, it's
a book!

Is this a joke?

No, it's a book!

DAD JOKES AND **PUNS**
**FROM INSTAGRAM'S LARGEST
DAD JOKES COMIC CREATOR**

Editor Florence Ward
Senior Designer David McDonald
Senior Aquisitions Editor Pete Jorgensen
Production Editor Siu Yin Chan
Production Controller Louise Minihane
Publishing Director Mark Searle

First American Edition, 2023
Published in the United States by DK Publishing
1745 Broadway, 20th Floor, New York, NY 10019

A catalog record for this book is available from the Library of Congress.
ISBN: 978-0-7440-7660-8

DK books are available at special discounts when purchased in bulk for
sales promotions, premiums, fund-raising, or educational use. For details,
contact: DK Publishing Special Markets, 1745 Broadway, 20th Floor, New
York, NY 10019. SpecialSales@dk.com

Printed and bound in Italy

For the curious

www.dk.com

This book was made with Forest
Stewardship Council™ certified paper—
one small step in DK's commitment to a
sustainable future. For more information
go to www.dk.com/our-green-pledge

CONTENTS

INTRODUCTION

At its inception, PunHub was simply a bit of fun on the commute to the office, applying silly jokes to cheesy stock photos I had used for previous jobs. Since then, it has blossomed into a huge community with well over 1 MILLION followers on the Instagram page alone!

The page really took off during the COVID-19 pandemic, with everyone trapped at home in need of a good laugh and something to smile about. The combination of outrageously painful jokes paired with the dead-behind-the-eyes look of the often unrelated stock photo models really struck a chord online. PunHub is a community-driven project with tons of ideas put forward each week. Only the best of the best are made into comics in the trademark PunHub style. The creations reach millions of people every week and have been reposted on social media by the likes of Snoop Dogg, Elon Musk and countless others. This book showcases the greatest hits of the online page whilst bringing plenty of print exclusives. This is @punhubonline – offline.

EMERGENCY ATTENTION

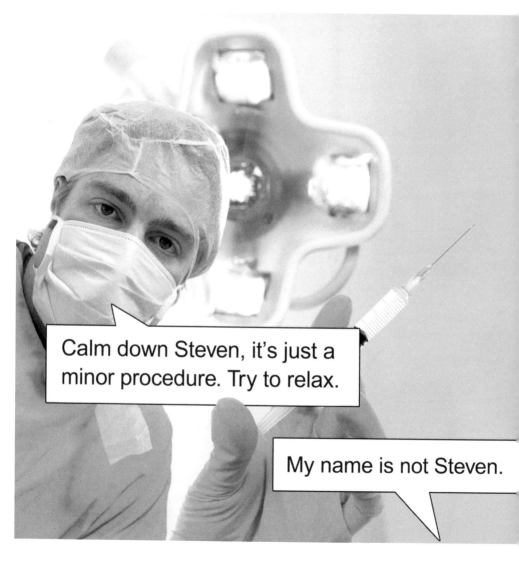

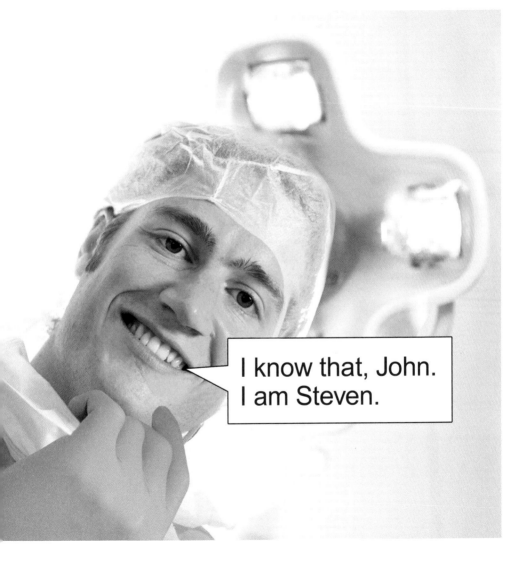

2

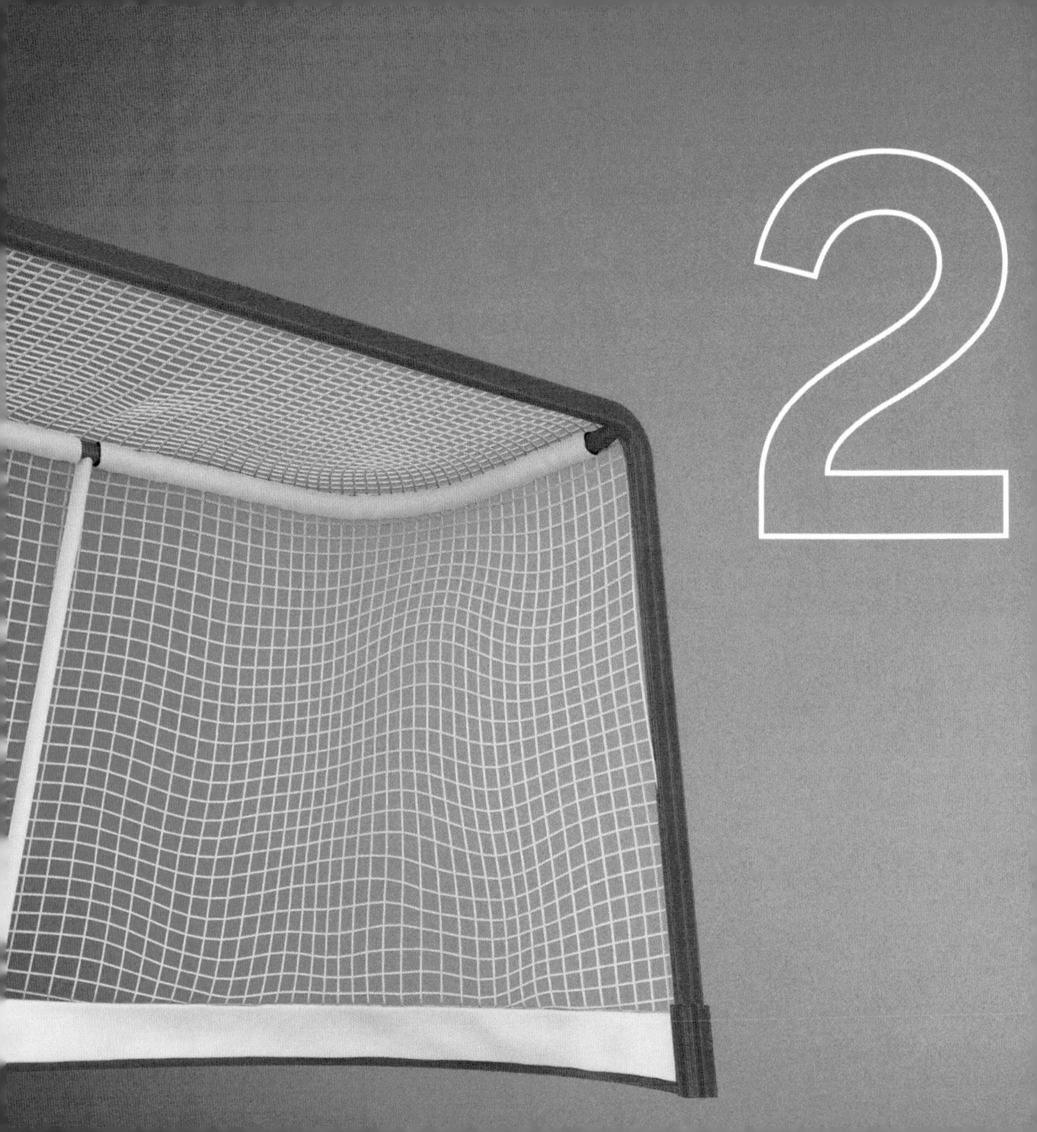

COUPLE
GOALS

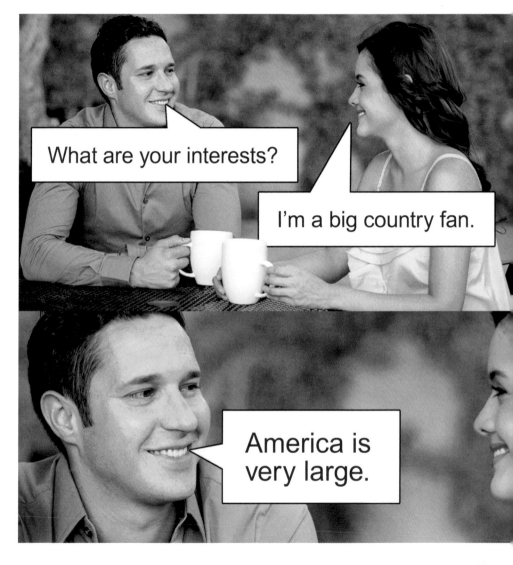

RETAIL
THERAPY

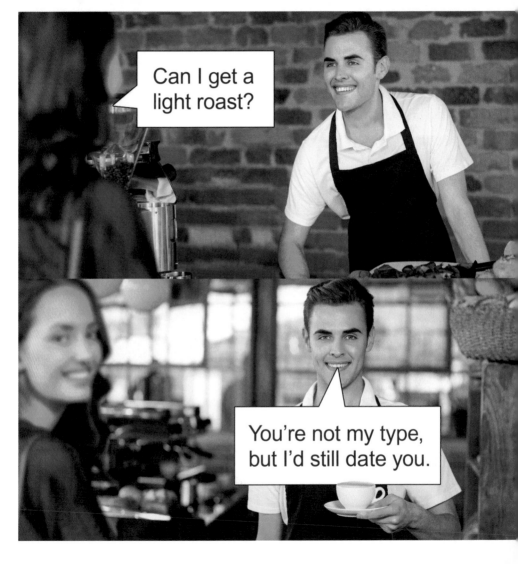

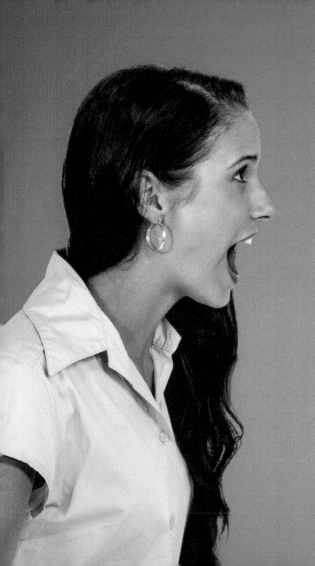

4

DAD
JOKES

5

RIDICULOUS
& RANDOM

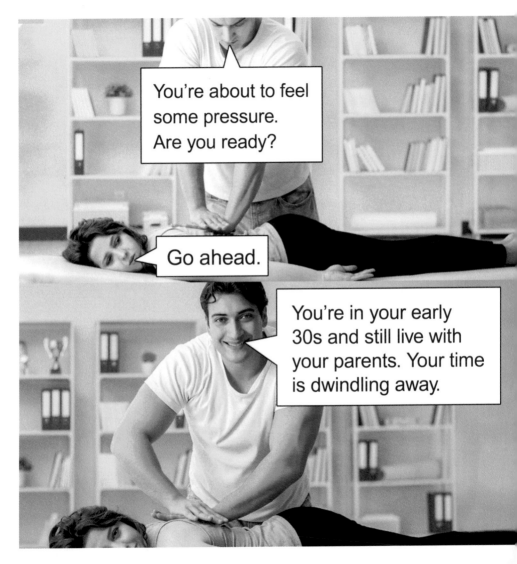

ON
THE JOB

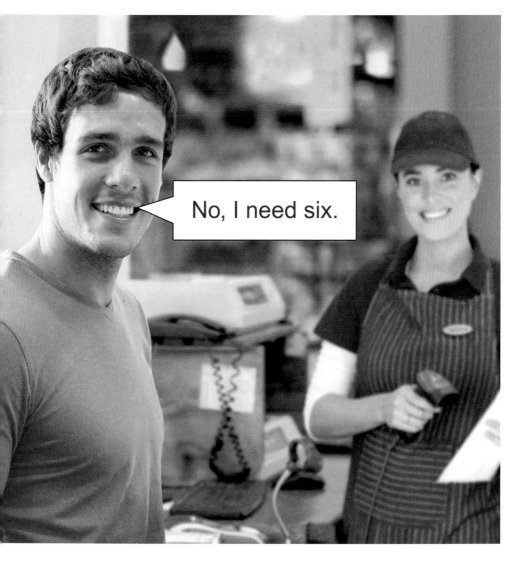

CRIME & PUNISHMENT

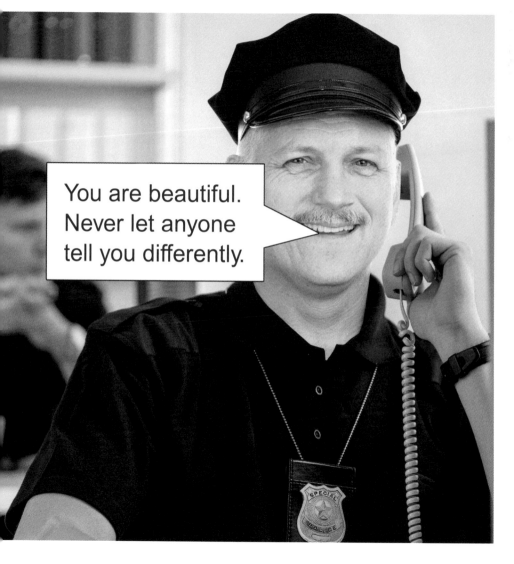

Joke Credits

14: I'm afraid the operation left you completely blind: Twitter: @shenthebird. **16: You need some contacts**: Instagram: @triggerology. **22-23: You have no patients:** Instagram: @triggerology. **32: Check you out? I already have a girlfriend:** Instagram: @triggerology. **33: Comfortable sir?:** Instagram: @pun_bible. **34: We should get dinner again:** Twitter: @MrJohnDarby. **36: I race cars:** Twitter: @sofarrsogud. **37: Are you finished?:** Pete Jorgensen. **38: Do you have any children?:** Twitter: @Kieransofar. **39: Bitten by a huge dog:** Twitter: @ItsAndyRyan. **40: Big country fan:** Twitter: @TheToddWilliams. **41: Yacht C is silent:** Instagram: @BadJokeBen. **43: March 1st:** Twitter: @TweetPotato314. **46: Oh no our neighbour died, who Ray?:** Twitter: @BigJDubz. **47: I think I have a crush on Beyonce:** Twitter: @Jeffw. **50: Wait, I can change:** Reddit: u/porichoygupto. **54: Is this gluten free?:** Instagram: @christopherashmanactor. **60: Winning an argument:** Twitter: @clichedout. **63: Is this train running on time?:** Twitter: @rebrafsim. **66: Light roast:** Instagram: @gogomemes. **68: Do you have any books on turtles?:** Twitter: @JokesWithMark. **79: Have you met my daughter Beth?:** Reddit: u/makka-pakka. **80-81: Yes, we arson:** Reddit: u/623fer. **84: Long story:** Reddit: u/deadalivecat. **86: Put the kids shoes on:** Instagram: @ciaranrk. **93: Thanks mailman:** Instagram: @pun_bible. **94: You herd me:** Reddit: u/baffledpanda. **97: Why do you call your horse Mayo?:** Twitter: @Kieransofar. **99: What is your favourite month?:** Twitter: @climaxximus. **101: Wait! I'm a talking tree!:** Twitter: @uncleduke1969. **107: Thereisnospacebar:** Reddit: u/TazocinTDS. **109: Second hand?:** Pete Jorgensen. **112: Hard drive:** Reddit: u/porichoygupto. **113 and cover: Can you type fast?:** Twitter: @MrJohnDarby. **114-115: Welcome to the library**: Instagram: @BadJokeBen. **116: Can you explain these gaps in your resume?:** Twitter: @patsatweetin. **122-123: Ammonia cleaner:** Twitter: @DadJokeMan. **130-131: Stop! I can't run anymore:** Twitter: @ThatMummyLife. **132: I would like to buy some weed, announce:** Twitter: @ItsAndyRyan. **134-135: Emergency attention:** Instagram: @gogomemes.

All other jokes are from @PunHub.

Picture Credits

The publisher would like to thank the following for their kind permission to reproduce their photographs:

(Key: a-above; b-below/bottom; c-centre; f-far; l-left; r-right; t-top)

1: iStock: tommy. **3:** iStock: tommy. **5:** iStock: tommy. **6:** iStock: tommy. **8-9:** Images repeated from (left to right) pages 12, 13, 16, 17, 26, 79, 39, 38, 41, 55, 27, 119, 68, 66, 67, 62, 69, 107. **10-11: Emergency Attention:** Dreamstime: Nyul (fl); Shutterstock: focal point (fr). **12: Call me an ambulance:** All images Dreamstime: Katarzyna Bialasiewicz. **13: Describe your symptoms:** All images Dreamstime: Elnur. **14: The operation left you completely blind:** Dreamstime: Nyul (tl); Dreamstime: Wavebreak Media Ltd (tr); Dreamstime: Vgstudio (tr); Dreamstime: Nyul (bl); Dreamstime: Wavebreak Media Ltd (br); Dreamstime: Vgstudio (br). **15: Your results are not great:** All images Dreamstime: Wavebreak Media Ltd (a). **16: You're going to need some contacts:** Dreamstime: Wavebreak Media Ltd (a); Dreamstime: Wavebreak Media Ltd (b). **17: She needs a crown:** iStock: Wavebreak Media Ltd (a); iStock: Wavebreak Media Ltd (b); Shutterstock: Val Lawless (bc). **18: I'm great, thanks:** iStock: Wavebreak Media Ltd (a); Dreamstime: Wavebreak Media Ltd (b); Dreamstime: Wavebreak Media Ltd (br). **19: Do you smoke or drink?:** All images Dreamstime: Monkey Business Images (tl); Lisa F. Young (tr); Monkey Business Images (bl); Lisa F. Young (br). **20: Try not to get aroused:** Shutterstock: Pop Paul-Catalin (tl); iStock: TerryJ (a); iStock: Catalin205 (bl); iStock: TerryJ (br). **21: This news won't be easy for you to hear:** All images Dreamstime: Elnur. **22-23: You have no patients:** Dreamstime: Nyul (fl); Dreamstime: Yuri Arcurs (cl); Shutterstock: focal point (cl); Dreamstime: Yuri Arcurs (cr); Dreamstime: Nyul (r); Shutterstock: focal point (fr). **24-25: Minor procedure:** Dreamstime: Hongqi Zhang (fl); Dreamstime: Toxawww (bc); Dreamstime: Hongqi Zhang (r); iStock: Wavebreakmedia (br). **26: I've not got all day:** Dreamstime: Monkey Business Images (tl); Dreamstime: Nyul (tr); Dreamstime: Nyul (tr); Dreamstime: Monkey Business Images (bl); Dreamstime: Nyul (br). **27: What happens after we die?:** Dreamstime: Nyul (tl); Dreamstime: Wavebreak Media Ltd (tr); Dreamstime: Vgstudio (tr); Dreamstime: Nyul (bl); Dreamstime: Wavebreak Media Ltd (br); Dreamstime: Vgstudio (br). **28-29: Couple Goals:** Both images iStock: Nerthuz. **30-31: We should go for a drink sometime:** Both images Dreamstime: Gstockstudio1. **32: Can I check you out?:** All images Dreamstime: Hongqi Zhang. **33: Comfortable sir?:** All images Dreamstime: Iakov Filimonov. **34: We should have dinner again:** Both images Dreamstime: prostockstudio. **35: You said we would go somewhere expensive for dinner:** Dreamstime: Carolyn Franks (a); Dreamstime: Pixattitude (a); Dreamstime: Carolyn Franks (b); Dreamstime: Pixattitude (bl); Dreamstime: Pixattitude (br). **36: I race cars:** All images Dreamstime: Antoniodiaz. **37: Are you finished?:** iStock: AVAVA [waitress]; all other images iStock: Antonio Guillem. **38: Bitten by a huge dog:** Both images Dreamstime: Gstockstudio1. **39: Do you have any children?:** Both images Dreamstime: Antonio Diaz. **40: Big country fan:** Both images Dreamstime: Antonio Diaz. **41: Yacht C is silent:** All images iStock: Antonio Guillem. **42: Quinoa:** Both images iStock: Wavebreakmedia. **43: March 1st:** Dreamstime: Adam Gregor (tr); Adam Gregor (bl); Kiriill Ryzhov (bfr). iStock: loco75 (tl); Aleksander Kaczmarek (tl); Aleksander Kaczmarek (br); Aleksander Kaczmarek (br). **44: Dirty things:** Background image iStock: Liudmila Chernetska. All other images Dreamstime: Wavebreakmedia. **45: What starts with S:** Both images iStock: nd3000. **46: Oh no our neighbour died, who Ray?:** Both Alamy Stock Image: Gpointstudios (photographer) and Cultura Creative Ltd (contributor). **47: I think I have a crush on Beyonce:** Both images Dreamstime: Gstockstudio1. **48: Have you seen the dog bowl?:** Dreamstime: Alexander Kharchenko (tl); Alexander Kharchenko (bl). iStock: iridi (bfl). All other images iStock: fizkes. **49: Gym instructor:** Both images Dreamstime: Iakov Filimonov. **50: Wait, I can change:** Background image iStock: si-f. All other images iStock: Wavebreakmedia. **51: Why did we need radios?:** Dreamstime: Fizkes (tl); Weiqing Xia (tl); Weiqing Xia (bl). iStock; fotostorm (a); Patrick Heagney (b); McIninch (bl). Shutterstock: Wavebreakmedia (bl). **52-53: Retail therapy:** Both images Dreamstime: Honqi Zhang (l); Wavebreakmedia (r). **54: Is this gluten free?:** Both images Dreamstime: Auremar. **55: I'd like to buy a muffin:** All images iStock: Antonio Diaz; osov (ac). **56-57: We'd like a table asap:** All images iStock: andresr. **58-59: I'm going to make you mine:** Dreamstime: Antonio Guillem (l); Phana Sitti (fr). Shutterstock: TTstudio (r); Antonio Guillem (cr); josefauer (cr); sajinnamu (cr); sajinnamu (fr); Antonio Guillem (fr). **60: Winning an argument:** Shutterstock: True Touch Lifestyle (a); Olena Yakobchuk (b). iStock: g_studio (tl). Dreamstime: Vgstudio (br). **61: How did you find your steak?:** Both images Dreamstime: Iakov Filimonov. **62: Is this good for insects?:** iStock: andresr. Dreamstime: Gradts (c). **63: Is this train running on time?:** Dreamstime: Auremar (tl); Auremar (bl); Lightpoet (br). iStock: Lightpoet (tr). **64: How do you think we keep the cars shiny?:** Both images Dreamstime: Puhhha. **65: Fill her up please:** Dreamstime: Studioloco (tl); Chernetskaya (tr); Chernetskaya (b); Studioloco (bl); Studioloco (bl). iStock: Blade_Kostas (br). **66: Light roast:** All images Dreamstime: Wavebreakmedia. **67: Can I get a wake-up call:** Dreamstime: Ukrphoto (tl); Kamil Macniak (tr). 123RF: elvinphoto (b). **68: Do you have any books on turtles?:** Both images Dreamstime: Iakov Filimonov. **69: How often do**

trains crash?: Dreamstime: Auremar (tl); Auremar (bl); Lightpoet (br). iStock: Lightpoet (tr). **70-71: Dad Jokes:** iStock: Wavebreakmedia (fl); Dreamstime: Piksel (r); iStock: Wavebreakmedia (ar). **72: Partner's waters broke:** iStock: fotostorm (tl); RichLegg (tr); fotostorm (bl). Shutterstock: Wavebreakmedia (tl); Wavebreakmedia (bl). **73: Would you like me to deliver the baby?:** Both images Dreamstime: Wavebreakmedia. **74-75: Awake until 3am with the baby:** Both images iStock: Wavebreakmedia. **76: Nothing rhymes with silver:** All images Dreamstime: Wavebreakmedia. **77: Santa is your dad:** All images Dreamstime: Wavebreakmedia. **78: Dad, have you brought my sunglasses?:** Dreamstime: Gpointstudio (a); Pavlo Rumiantsev (bl). iStock: Gpointstudio (b). **79: Have you met my daughter Beth?:** All images iStock: monkeybusinessimages. **80-81: Yes, we arson:** Dreamstime: Dale Stork (l); Andreadonetti (cl); Dale Stork (r). iStock: monkeybusinessimages (cl); monkeybusinessimages (cr). **82: Mum, I'm going to be Frank with you:** iStock: fizkes (a). Dreamstime: Wavebreakmedia (b). **83: Daddy, why is the food cold?:** Both images Dreamstime: Wavebreakmedia. **84: Long story:** Both images Dreamstime: Prostockstudio. **85: Dad, do you know total eclipse?:** Dreamstime: Gpointstudio (a). iStock: Gpointstudio (b). **86: Put the kids shoes on:** Dreamstime: Piksel (tr); Piksel (br). All other images iStock: Wavebreakmedia. **87: Headlice:** All images Dreamstime: Wavebreakmedia. **88-89: Can you wake the kids up?:** Both images Dreamstime: Antonio Guillem. **90-91: Ridiculous and Random:** Alamy Stock Photo: fStop Images GmbH (fl). Dreamstime: Vgstudio (fl). All other images iStock: 4x6. **92: Do you need me to sign?:** Both images Dreamstime: Katarzyna Bialasiewicz. **93: Thanks mailman:** All images Shutterstock: Phovoir. **94: You herd me:** Getty Images: Peter Cade (a); Peter Cade (b). iStock: GlobalP (tr). **95: That's it boss, all 60 lambs:** Alamy Stock Photo: Wayne Hutchinson (a). iStock: nycshooter (tr). Dreamstime: Wirestock (bl). Shutterstock: Aneta Jungerova (bl). **96: I am well:** iStock: kunchauniub (a); kunchauniub (b). Dreamstime: Studio Loco (a). Shutterstock: Studio Loco (a). **97: Why do you curl your horse Mayo?:** Both images iStock: Emir Memedovski. **98: Perfect date:** Both images Dreamstime: Antonio Diaz. **99: What is your favourite month? July, Why July?:** Both images iStock: Antonio Guillem. **100: Abundance:** All images iStock: Rich Legg. **101: Wait! I'm a talking tree! Dialogue:** iStock: Simonkr (a); Simonkr (b); 4x6 (tr); 4x6 (br). 102-103: Air support: Alamy Stock Photo: PJF Military Collection (l); Alamy Stock Photo: PJF Military Collection (r). iStock: PeopleImages (l). Dreamstime: Alexey Novikov (r). **104: You're about to feel a little pressure:** Both images Dreamstime: Elnur. **105: It's on the house:** Dreamstime: Aliaksandr Nikitsin (b);

Steven Cukrov (c). iStock: dem10; Rattasak (tr). All other images Dreamstime: Ljupco. **106: Big metal fan:** Both images Dreamstime: Matthew Trommer. **107: Thereisnospacebar:** Dreamstime: Vgstudio (bl). All other images are Alamy Stock Photo: Caspar Benson - Contributor fStop Images GmbH. **108: Humans eat more nuts than squirrels:** Both images iStock: Antonio Guillem. **109: Second hand?:** Dreamstime: Chernetskaya (cl). All other images are Dreamstime: Monkey Business Images. **110-111: On the Job:** Both images Dreamstime: Fizkes (fl); Ambro10 (fr). **112: Hard drive:** Shutterstock: Pressmaster (a). All other images Shutterstock: studioloco. **113: Can you type fast?:** Both images Dreamstime: Fizkes. **114-115: Welcome to the library:** Dreamstime: Photographerlondon (cr); Sharon Yanai (l); Sharon Yanai (r); Didecs (l); Didecs (r). Shutterstock: Pathdoc (a); Pathdoc (b); Sirtravelalot. **116: Can you explain these gaps in your resume?:** Dreamstime: Ambro10 (bc). All other images Dreamstime: Arne9001. **117: Do you think you will be suited for the role?:** All images iStock: Antonio Guillem. **118: Why are you shaking?:** Both images iStock: ismagilov. **119: Quietest employee:** Dreamstime: Vgstudio (bc). All other images iStock: Drazen_. **120: Too weak notice:** iStock: Venerable (a); Venerable (b); londoneye (tr); londoneye (tr). All other images Dreamstime: Jose Manuel Gelpi Diaz. **121: Turn the car on:** All images iStock: Estradaanton. **122-123: Ammonia cleaner:** Dreamstime: Christi Tolbert (c). iStock: g_studio (fl). Shutterstock: Syda Productions (c); wavebreakmedia (r); Vgstudio (fl); Vgstudio (fr). **124: This says otherwise:** All images Dreamstime: Anna Kosolapova. **125: What has four letters:** All images iStock: Wavebreakmedia. **126-127: Chainsaws:** All images Dreamstime: Hongqi Zhang. **128-129: Crime and Punishment:** Both images Dreamstime: Lisa F. Young (fl); Andrey Popov (fr). **130-131: Stop! I can't run anymore:** iStock: 4x6 (fl); 4x6 (cr). Dreamstime: Andrey Popov (cl); Andrey Popov (fr). **132: I would like to buy some weed, announce:** All images Dreamstime: Felix Mizioznikov (tr); Rtdesignstudio (tr). All other images Dreamstime: Kurhan. **133: How high are you?:** Both images Dreamstime: Lisa F. Young. **134-135: Emergency attention:** 123RF: undrey (a); undrey (b). Alamy Stock Photo: Oliver Floerke (bl). Dreamstime: Katarzyna Bialasiewicz (a); Lisa F. Young (a); Lisa F. Young (b). **136: I have contacts:** All images Dreamstime: Lisa F. Young. **137: Hummus side:** Dreamstime: Lisa F. Young (b). All other images iStock: JackF. **138-139: The thief stole $50,000 of fuel:** Dreamstime: Chernetskaya (fl); Lisa F. Young (cl); Chernetskaya (cr); Lisa F. Young (fr).

I would like to thank all the followers of the PunHub channels that made this book a reality. Without your consistent engagement, joke submissions and all-around good vibes this would never have been possible. A huge thanks for all the joke contributions to the book, I would really recommend checking out the socials listed within the credits page for more amazing writing from some very funny people. A shoutout to my publisher for seeing the potential in the page, in particular Pete Jorgensen, who himself has contributed several jokes to the book and etched his name in to PunHub folklore forever.

Last and most certainly not least, I would like to thank the real star of the show; my wife for being extremely supportive throughout both the growth of the page and whilst putting together this book. Being my sounding board for the many hundreds of terrible jokes throughout the years has ensured that as the followers of the page say "PunHub doesn't miss" I hope your loved the book and I look forward to putting out the next one!